T0147171

Youth Truth

Why You Can Trust the Bible

Kathleen Wood

WESTBOW
PRESS®
A DIVISION OF THOMAS NELSON
& ZONDERVAN

WestBow Press books may be ordered through
booksellers or by contacting:

WestBow Press
A Division of Thomas Nelson & Zondervan
1663 Liberty Drive
Bloomington, IN 47403
www.westbowpress.com
1 (866) 928-1240

Scripture taken from the New King James Version®. Copyright ©
1982 by Thomas Nelson. Used by permission. All rights reserved.

ISBN: 978-1-9736-7668-3 (sc)
ISBN: 978-1-9736-7667-6 (e)

Library of Congress Control Number: 2019915709

Print information available on the last page.

WestBow Press rev. date: 10/04/2019

I dedicate this book first to the Lord Jesus Christ, who has changed my life, healed my body, and saved my soul. He continues to show great mercy and kindness to me, giving me strength each day by His Spirit.

I also dedicate this book to my dear grandchildren, Ava, Scarlett, and Katharine, so that they too may know there is reason to believe the truth about God, Jesus, and the Bible and that, knowing this, they will walk with the Lord all their days.

Contents

Preface xi
1: What Is the Bible? 1
  In the Beginning 2
  What Are the Old and New Testaments? 3
  Reliability of Old Testament Scripture 4
  New Testament Scripture 5
  The Shocking Last Book 9
  The Language of the Bible 12
  Other Resources for Study 13
2: What about Prophecy? 17
  Mathematical Implications and Probability 18
  Bible Prophecy Reveals God 20
  Example 1: It's a Big Deal! 21
    Then What Happened? 23
    I Told You So! 25
    So What? 29
  Example 2: Who Knew? 31
    Daniel and the King's Dream 31
    A Bad Dream 32
    Another God Dream 39
    How Do I Interpret This? 39

Example 3: Jesus, the Fulfillment of Prophecy
    (or Who Is This Guy, Anyway?)................40
    Didn't I Tell You? *42*
    Do the Math *43*
3: Wait, There's More! *The Bible and the Sciences* ..47
    Archeology 47
    Hittites, Horites, and Horror 48
        The Hittite Culture *48*
        The Horites *49*
        A Worldwide Flood *50*
    To Conclude..51
    Biology and The God of Life 51
        The DNA Blueprint *53*
    There's an App for That....................................54
    It's All About You! 55
        The Wonder of Blood *57*
    The Bible in Geology 58
    What Anthropologists Tell Us 59
    Other Scientific Information that Verifies the
        Bible 60
        The Bethlehem Star *62*
4: The Resurrection of Christ 65
    Questions for Further Thought 67
        Tortured for Truth 69
    Authenticity of History....................................70
    Consider...72
    Eyewitness Accounts.......................................73
        The Embarrassing Details *73*
        Eye Spy *76*
        Not a Game! *78*

Important to Know..81
Councils and Creeds...82
The Persecuted Church 85
In Conclusion 87
References and Sermon Notes 89
About the Author 95

Preface

The purpose of this book is to impress upon young people that the Bible holds truth that is relevant today. I want to pass on this knowledge and the truth of the Bible to the next generation. I hope you, the reader, will understand through the pages of this short biblical overview that God indeed exists and that He has a good purpose and plan for your life.

The Bible claims that God created you. He loves you no matter who you are, where you live, or what you've done. This truth gives hope to millions who are hurting, as well as confidence with which to approach the future.

From my more than twenty years of experience as a teacher, I know many schools try to prepare students for a successful future by educating them in areas they will need in life—math, science, reading, social studies. Yet they do not teach or prepare students for the most important part of life: spiritual understanding. Without spiritual understanding, it is as though you are making life decisions in the dark.

It is natural to be afraid of the dark. Without light, you cannot see. Something might be there to trip you or hurt you in some way. How could you know? But if there were a light to turn on, you could see clearly. You could make decisions about where to go and what to do.

Psalm 119, verse 105 says, "Thy word, O Lord, is a lamp unto my feet and a light unto my path." God has provided a light for our spiritual understanding in the Bible. He offers this light to everyone if we ask Him and receive it. I sincerely hope that through knowing more about the Bible you will be encouraged to find out more and search for God's direction on your life journey.

Although the information I present in this book is by no means exhaustive, I have attempted to provide enough facts so that any thinking person will be aware that the Bible is not just myth and fiction. Unless otherwise noted I have used the New King James version consistently throughout this book. It is my belief that the Bible holds significant nuggets of truth relevant for the youth of today and shows there is reason to believe.

1: What Is the Bible?

The Bible is a collection of sixty-six books written more than 1,500 years ago. The oldest documented authentic ancient scripture fragments are called the Dead Sea Scrolls. These date back to 250 BCE. That is more than 2,250 years old!

The authors of these books—the manuscripts that we now call the Bible—were diverse. They came from different geographic locations, lived in different cultures with differing traditions, and were of diverse ethnicities. There are forty-five authors represented in the Bible. Their writings were often controversial in their time. Many are just as controversial today.

The Bible contains variety of writing styles and genres. There are poems, songs, prayers such as in the psalms of King David, and records of genealogy. There are letters, prophecies, moral teachings, and chronology.

However, these sixty-six books written over 2,500 years ago have one common theme, which becomes more evident as you read more of the Bible. The Bible claims there is a loving God who cares for each of us. He is a personal God desperately wanting a relationship with us, His crowning creation. The details of God's interaction with humankind can be clearly seen throughout the scripture writings.

In the Beginning

Taken as a whole, the Bible describes the creation of the world, including human beings. It explains how God created the earth and us as whole and good, with humankind created in God's own image. This means that He gave us a free will to think, decide, and choose. He did not mean for us to be robots who are not able to alter their destinies. While animals have instincts that drive them, human behavior is more complex with decision-making and motivation as thinking, self-analytical creatures. The first chapters of Genesis explain how and why the first humans rebelled from God's directions and chose their own ways rather than God's way. This account describes human suffering, God's intervention, and a promise that all would be made right again one day through God's Son. Whereas humans now have a sinful attribute, the God-man, Jesus, would not. Therefore, He would be the Messiah given for our restoration and a plan for the future of earth.

What Are the Old and New Testaments?

The Bible is divided into two parts: the Old and New Covenants. These are often called the Old Testament and the New Testament.

The Old Testament contains the early history of humankind and the origins and promises of God to those fathers of faith who would trust and follow Him. It contains history of the Jewish nation, Israel, and the books of Moses, which gave us the Ten Commandments and the Jewish Law. The Old Testament also contains prophetic writings and psalms as well as proverbs and chronicles of kings and judges during Israel's early history.

The prophets foretold things that would happen. These prophecies explained to all who would listen why God behaved the way He did, and what He wanted and why. They are insights, for they reveal more about God's character. Even today, these many prophetic writings are studied by Christians and Jews alike. They include books from Isaiah, Jeremiah, Hosea, Amos, Obadiah, Daniel, and others. More about the Old Covenant will be discussed in the section on Bible prophecy so readers can see that, indeed, the things that were foretold have and will come to pass with an incredible accuracy only God can know!

In addition, the Old Testament contains writings about the origins of the universe, the creation of the world, the first human beings, God's purposes, and the responses to His creation. It clearly shows that humans exercise free will and reveals the first sin, the first murder, deceptions and lies, moral law, and God's judgment as well as His forgiveness. The Old Testament traces the origins of the Jewish nation and the history of the Arab people through a man named Abraham. He is called the father of many nations. Indeed, this is historically and undeniably true of the Arab people as well as the Jewish people, who both trace their ancestry through Father Abraham.

Reliability of Old Testament Scripture

Much of the ancient historic writings in the Old Testament have been well studied and proven accurate in the field of archaeology as well as in other branches of the sciences. Archaeological discoveries reveal precise details exactly as the Bible described them, giving authenticity and validity to the Bible's ancient historic writings. We will examine a few of these findings.

For example, lists of regional wars from biblical accounts have provided specific dates, names of kings, particular areas, and battles. As archaeologists discovered more and more in their explorations by digging in the specific areas described in the Bible, they found various cities and cultures with the precise details as the Bible describes. Many of these findings were also preserved in documentation from these periods, such as written tablets or monuments. These archaeological finds verify precise details as given in scripture. Therefore, the Bible has proven a reliable resource for this branch of science for the purpose of unearthing ancient history. We will examine some specific examples in the section of this book on sciences.

New Testament Scripture

The books of the New Testament or New Covenant begin with the birth of Jesus in the writings of Matthew. Matthew was a real person and one of Jesus's close disciples. He was a tax collector before he became a follower, or disciple, of Jesus. A lot of important genealogical information tracing Jesus back through Abraham, Isaac and Jacob, King David, and so forth is recorded in Matthew's book. Jesus's birth, life, and ministry are also described as seen and experienced through the eyes of this disciple.

The other Gospel writings include Mark's, Luke's, and John's. These books in the New Testament complete a section known as the Gospels. Gospel means "good news." It is a fitting description for the presentation of the long-awaited Messiah, the promised Savior, who will reign, deliver, and forgive. *Yeshua* is the Hebrew word for Jesus. *Jesus* means "God saves" in the Hebrew language. The term *Christ* means "anointed one." Therefore, all these terms describe Jesus, who is called Christ. We will see how every one of these terms fits incredibly into what the Old Testament prophets foretold of the Messiah and how amazingly accurately Jesus fulfilled these glimpses into the future with His birth, life, and death.

One example of this uncanny prediction, the coming of Christ, was foretold in chapter 53 of the writings of Isaiah. It is an undeniably accurate description of Jesus as He suffered death by crucifixion. At the time of the prophet Isaiah, crucifixions had not been invented. Yet this prophet writes his description vividly and unmistakably. How did he know?

Another example is that of Daniel. Daniel shares his visions and dreams regarding future world events and the Messiah's reign. We will examine how—according to historical records—these visions and dreams of Daniel did in fact come to pass. The succession of world leaders and ruling nations was so accurately predicted into the future that I wouldn't be surprised if you get chills reading it.

Writings of Mathew, Mark, and John are testimonial in nature. This means their reports record what they had heard and witnessed. They also mention events that happened during their time with Jesus. They come from the perspective of knowing Jesus firsthand. They watched him. They worked with him. They walked and talked with Jesus. They asked many questions during Yeshua's brief life of approximately thirty-three years. Jesus's actual ministry to those around Him spanned only the last three of those years.

Luke's Gospel account is thought by scholars to be the written account as dictated later by another disciple. Luke was a physician with literary skills, which not all people of that day possessed. If another illiterate disciple asked Luke to write the account, it contains that perspective as well. Luke was also much younger than most of the other disciples, possibly only tagging along and taking notes from what he saw and heard.

Ending each testimony of all four Gospels is a description of Jesus's final hours. Their sad and bewildered descriptions give us details of Jesus's excruciating death, His suffering on the cross, His burial, and His resurrection. The disciples honestly conveyed their sadness and horror as they witnessed their Messiah being turned over to Rome, His beating, and then His hanging helplessly on a Roman cross. Brokenhearted and fearful, the disciples hid from zealot Jewish leaders who called Jesus a fraud. They were also afraid for their own lives, knowing that the same Roman guards and leaders who crucified Christ were looking for His disciples as well.

Does that sound exciting? Find out more by reading these Gospel accounts.

And these same cowering disciples tell how they were convinced of Jesus's miraculous return to life. They could not keep silent when they saw with their own eyes the risen Savior!

Jesus had told them He would rise on the third day. The ancient prophets had foretold it. They just did not understand. Jesus did exactly as He said He would do. Though doubts and fears overwhelmed the disciples initially, they became true believers through a series of appearances by the resurrected Christ over several days.

Too amazing to be true? Study more about how history was changed by these events.

These same fearful disciples were transformed by the power of this risen Christ. More on this subject will be discussed in a later section about the Resurrection.

The testimony of those to whom Jesus appeared after His death and resurrection overturned the entire known world. The book of Acts describes what transpired afterward. God proved by His Spirit that He was in this adventure with the new believers. Word spread of this miraculous Jesus and His resurrection. As news traveled, it changed many lives. The Christian Gospel continues to change lives today. I am one He has changed.

However, these events brought believers great persecution at the hands of those who felt threatened by a new religion and by its growing number of followers. How could they control something like this, a king with such great power? Even so, "the Way"—as it was sometimes called—thrived despite attempts to silence the disciples' preaching. (See Acts 9:12 and 22:4)

Christianity is still thriving today, with an estimated three billion followers worldwide. Though calls to silence the church in today's culture persist and violent persecution in many parts of the world exists, Jesus's promise to His followers is recorded in Matthew 16:18: "The gates of Hades shall not prevail against it." referring to the His church. He assures us that He has His eye on His beloved children, often referred to as the body of Christ in the world today.

The rest of the exciting New Testament describes the birth of what is now called Christianity, how God dealt with those who hear the Gospel, the protection of God of His message and people, letters written by the apostles to other fellow believers, and the last book of the New Testament, Revelation.

The Shocking Last Book

This book is also referred to as the Revelation of Jesus to His beloved apostle John. It is full of imagery and insights regarding the end times. The persecutors of the church had tried to boil

John in oil to kill him. However, they could not cause this man of God to die. He was the oldest living apostle at the time because the rest had been martyred. After the attempt to boil him in oil failed, John was exiled to an isle called Patmos. It was there that John wrote the most amazing account of what seem to be future events. It comforts and admonishes believers to this day. It describes what will happen in the end of the age and gives hope and encouragement to those who suffer for the cause of Christ. Revelations describes the rise of the Antichrist and the return of Jesus Christ, warns of God's wrath, encourages believers with the glories awaiting them, and admonishes Christians to remain faithful unto the very end.

It is shocking in places because, up to now, many of the book's detailed descriptions could not have been possible. Yet, today with current technology these descriptions often read like current events. John's visions describe a mandatory marking or identification of all individuals. It is called the mark of the beast, a worldwide system of accounting for masses of people. This mark would keep track of financial and personal information, eventually by a world leader called the Antichrist. This leader would come on the scene to bring about global unity, supposedly in peace and goodness. Yet the sinister nature of this one who is the very opposite of the Lord Jesus Christ would be realized by many too late. Currently, a radio frequency identification chip, or RFC, is used for tracking pets and for employees in some parts of the world.

Could this serve the purpose described in Revelation? A global system of identification could allow everyone to be tracked and accounted for with little personal control over buying and selling without the prescribed chip or mark.

The Bible clearly predicts that there would be a setting up of world powers and the rise of an Antichrist, a world ruler, who comes in peacefully at first. But he will take demonic control, ushering in a great worldwide tribulation period. His hatred for humankind and the God who created us is unmatched. His true desire is not peace and unity but destruction, enslavement, and pure evil. The Bible describes this reign of evil dictatorship as a time unlike any other on the earth and unlike any that ever will be again. Judgements against all those who have rejected God's ways and His Son, Jesus, will be poured out during this time.

While those who remain faithful to the Lord may suffer, they will be preserved and kept for the glories that await them at the return of Christ to set up His earthly kingdom. The earth will be renewed. True justice and righteousness will reign over all the earth. All evil will be subdued. This is the hope of nations. Hymn lyrics refer to this hope. Artists have dreamed of it for centuries. "The Peaceable Kingdom" by renowned artist Edward

Hicks is one such example. Revelation chapter 21 gives a description.

The Language of the Bible

The Bible was originally written in three languages. They are Hebrew, Aramaic, and Greek, depending on the time period of the writing. Today we have versions of the texts in every major known language. But the organization Wycliff Translators and other groups have endeavored to make the scriptures accessible to even the most remote tribes and population groups on the face of the earth, a huge task.

Translations from the original texts are by far the best and most accurate way to read and study the scriptures. I personally recommend two such translations for this purpose. The New King James Version, or NKJV, is a revised form of the original King James Bible. It eliminates the thees and thous of the older King James version, yet the text remains true to the original manuscripts. It is therefore easier for modern readers to understand without archaic language patterns. Another recommended translation is the NASV, or New American Standard Version. The translators for this version returned to the original manuscripts and, since the major discovery of the Dead Sea Scrolls, ensured the most accurate modern translation possible. It, too, provides easier reading in our modern age without sacrificing accuracy.

Other representations have been printed. The popular Living Bible is a not a translation but rather a paraphrased version. Paraphrasing is when someone puts into his or her own words what has been said by someone else. I say I am happy, for example. You might paraphrase me to say I am in a good mood. It is similar but not exact. The Message is another version that has become popular and readily available. This version reads like a novel story but has many alterations to authentic scripture. Other versions have also become popularized.

However, if the Bible one reads is not a translation that scholars and linguistic experts, as well as experts from every related field, have thoroughly scrutinized and provided, it is unlikely to represent an accurate and meaningful translation of authentic scriptures as they were originally written. Without an accurate translation, the key concepts and doctrines from the original text may be lost. At the same time, referring to additional versions might be helpful to our understanding when reading an authentic translation as well.

Other Resources for Study

A number of additional resources besides the Bible itself can be useful tools to help you achieve a good overall understanding while reading and studying the Bible. These include Bible references, Bible dictionaries, biblical encyclopedias, and Bible commentaries and concordances. These tools are often helpful to explain names, dates, and references for certain concepts in scripture, as well as cultural or historic context.

In addition, many fine subject matter bible studies exist in today's marketplace, both online and in print. Many churches and Christian organizations offer courses, some completely free or available for a small donation to cover costs. Practically every church, regardless of denomination, is making it easier to study scripture through the use of technology, offering online streaming sermons, Bible teachings, study guides, and more.

Never has the Bible been more available to the masses than it is today. Once only read by priests and kings, scripture is now available to anyone in the world. Audio recordings of the Bible and listening devices allow even illiterate or moderate readers to access God's word.

The lyrics of an old hymn express the longing of our hearts to hear and know more about Jesus.

"Tell Me the Stories of Jesus"

Tell me the stories of Jesus I love to hear,
Things I would ask Him if He were here.
Scenes by the wayside, tales of the sea,
Stories of Jesus, tell them to me.
First let me hear how the children stood round
    his knee,
And I shall fancy his blessing resting on me,
Words full of kindness, deeds full of grace,
All in the love light of Jesus's face.

          —Lyrics by William H. Parker, 1885

2: What about Prophecy?

Although some have tried to predict the future through tarot cards, tea leaves, astrological signs, or even psychic channeling, these methods are only accurate about 50 percent of the time. That is no more convincing than the toss of a coin. It's either heads, you win or tails, you lose. And both are equally possible. It is a safe bet that the outcome will certainly be one of those two possibilities. To pick one of the two possibilities means you have a 50 percent chance of getting it right.

However, Bible prophecy has an accuracy rate that is far superior. We will look at some specific examples. We will see that prophecies given centuries before the predicted event took place have been proven to be 100 percent accurate 100 percent of the time! Even more amazing is that the details described in these prophecies came to pass precisely without fail in 100 percent of the cases. Would you expect anything less if someone claimed to speak from God?

One-fourth of the Bible is predictive. This means that the writings described events that would happen at some future time. Many of these predictive prophecies stated specific information such as the names of nations, groups of people, regions, specific kings, and reigns of rulers as well as the events themselves.

Mathematical Implications and Probability

Mathematics is important here. The rate of accuracy for Bible prophecy points to a God who is all knowing, all powerful, and loving, a caring God who reveals secret things to His creation with good intent. No human being could possibly know the future with such clarity and precision as scriptural writings have shown. We will look at the mathematical probabilities of a few prophetic writings that have come to pass exactly and precisely as described thousands of years before occurring. The chances of that happening are well outside the standard deviation statistically speaking. In other words, it is mathematically impossible to be coincidental.

There are warnings, admonitions, directions, encouragement, and hope in scriptural prophecies. The uncanny accuracy of Bible prophecy also points to the reliability and accuracy of the scripture in other respects. We shall examine this evidence. In the following pages, we will investigate the claims to see if indeed there truly is an all-knowing deity who reveals secrets to mere mortals.

The lyrics of a song entitled "Maybe There Is a God," sung by gifted Christian musician, Sara Groves, reminds me of young people today seeking meaning and searching to find out what, if anything, is life all about:

"I'm trying to work things out.
I'm trying to comprehend.
Am I the chance result
Of some great accident?
I hear a rhythm call me,
The echo of a grand design."

"And I have never prayed a lot
But maybe there's a loving God."

The song goes on to explain how the mere acts of questioning, searching, and thinking open the door to explore possibilities.

I hope you will fully consider the possibilities of what the scriptures tell us and of what I present in this book.

Here is the Bible's explanation of how it was written from the Apostle Peter.

"... no prophecy of the scripture is of any private interpretation. For the prophecy never came by the will of man; but holy men of God spoke as they were moved by the Holy Spirit" (2 Pet. 1:20).

Bible Prophecy Reveals God

The authors of the Bible claimed their words and understanding of the future came to them by divine revelation. In other words, they claimed that these prophetic revelations came directly from God and were written down by the hand of man. They told of dreams, visions, and visitations by angelic beings.

Yet, this explanation is only worth considering if what they claim was revealed by God proves to be clearly correct and without error. Trust in a "thus saith the Lord" means that the omniscient God, knowing all things past, present, and future, Jehovah God of the Bible, Maker of the Universe, Creator God, God of Truth, is revealing something that He wants His creation to understand. It will not be false. He cannot lie. He will not mislead us, because He is beneficent, loving, and kind. It will not be a mistake, because this God knows everything. It will come to pass exactly and precisely how God describes. Otherwise, we cannot point to it as coming from this kind of god. Only a God like this would be able to know things and reveal them to His holy prophets in such a divine way for the benefit and edification of all people.

Though many consider parts of the Bible's teachings to be controversial, we do know from mathematics, astronomy, technology, history, archeology, and other sciences that claims of these prophetic writers have come to pass exactly, precisely, and astoundingly accurately as they were described in the writings. These have been authenticated sometimes to the point of amazement. I will describe three such prophecies to you. Then you, the reader, can see for yourself.

We must look at this with a logical conclusion: if the Bible is 100 percent accurate and predicted at the time of its writing events that were fulfilled far in the future, the Bible has credibility in what it tells us.

A full one-fourth of the Bible's sixty-six books is predictive in nature. These writings describe events and explain God's dealings with humankind. All of the predicted events have not happened yet. But many were given centuries before and have now been fulfilled.

Example 1: It's a Big Deal!

Israel is my first example. We can call it exhibit A for the purpose of explanation. Delivered through Moses from Egyptian slavery, these ancient people called the Jews became the tiny nation of Israel. Moses and other prophets warned from the beginning that Israel could fall away from its holy covenant relationship with their God, Jehovah. Even though He did the miraculous to display His love and deliverance for the Jewish people, they turned aside to worship the gods of other nations surrounding them.

Over many years of warnings and pleading with His people through the prophets, God finally brought the consequences, or judgements, He had said would happen because of their sin and spiritual adultery. As you read through the Old Testament and its prophetic books, the imagery described is often that of a love relationship. Like a relationship between a faithful husband and an unfaithful wife, God describes His covenant of faithful love for His unfaithful people.

The prophet Hosea even describes this heartbreak of God Almighty as a divorce. The prophet Hosea was married to an unfaithful wife, a prostitute, who kept leaving him for other men. The imagery here cannot be mistaken.

We read of God pleading with His people over the centuries under many different prophets and kings. They were warned that they would lose the land God had promised their forefathers, Abraham, Isaac, and Jacob. God described how they would be scattered all over the world because of their disobedience and rebellion toward Him.

God had given a glimpse of Himself, His justice, and His mercy in the law, also known as the Ten Commandments. These laws would be an example of what God is like for the world to see. But instead of being an example, the Jewish people neither kept the laws of God nor honored those whom

God had sent them for correction and reproof. He wanted to bring them back on track. God's intent was to warn them of the dire consequences that were ahead if they continued in their sin. They were acting no differently than the pagan nations around them.

Then What Happened?

It is truly tragic when you think of this. The book of Jeremiah, parts of the book of Isaiah, and other prophetic books describe the devastation as the Babylonian armies conquered Jerusalem, the Jews' holiest city. History shows that the warnings and prophetic predictions came true.

At the time of the Babylonian captivity, some educated, healthy Jews were also taken as slaves to serve in Babylon. This is described in the book of Daniel. Daniel was one whose life was spared when he was taken as a captive. We will speak more about this amazing young person later. But God's people indeed lost the land they were promised. The temple was destroyed. Their lives were lost, or they were enslaved. Destruction of their entire culture and heritage was imminent. Genocide was threatened.

Yet, during the reign of King Cyrus, Jerusalem was allowed to be rebuilt. The book of Nehemiah describes this in detail as well. And history proves that it, too, came to pass. The tragedy and the fulfillment of these prophecies about Israel and the Jewish captivity in Babylon truly are sad. They have a balance, however.

The joy of restoration in a regathering was also what God promised. Israel would become a nation again in the latter days. God described that after all these terrible things came to pass, He would gather the Jewish people again to the land of Israel. They would stream in from all over the world.

God's loving and miraculous regathering of the Jewish people into the land of Israel would be a sign to them. It would be an assurance that they were still His covenant people. It would comfort them in their suffering to know that God would still be their God. And further, it would be a witness for all people in the world that this God was God alone and true to His word.

The fact that Israel is regathered from wherever they were scattered is a sign to the whole world that God is truly God! Now we know from history that Israel indeed lost her land and was overcome by the Babylonian Empire in 589 BC. The events as described through prophecy actually happened. The capital of Jerusalem was destroyed, and many were slaughtered or starved. Through many centuries the Jews did not have a homeland. The popular musical *Fiddler on the Roof* tells a story about a Jewish community being driven out of the other nations where they resided after their homeland was invaded. Indeed, the Jewish people were scattered all over the world.

Looking forward to the present day, we view the historical account in the announcement of the United Nations after World War II. Israel again became a nation. The God who told them He would regather them again made certain it happened. The date of May 14, 1948 is famous as the declaration of Israel's rebirth. Former U.S. President Harry Truman concurred. The Balfour Declaration that gave a homeland back to the Jewish people was realized, as was foretold in scripture centuries prior.

So, to our amazement, it was decided after World War II by the United Nations that the Jewish people would again have the land of Israel as their homeland. The end of Hitler's diabolical attempt to systematically eliminate the Jews had failed. Jewish people streamed into Israel from all over the world. The ancient land of Israel was again declared a Jewish nation. Not only that, but the ancient Hebrew language was revived! It is now their official language and used daily.

I Told You So!

Here is a brief overview from the Old Testament scriptures about the things I have just described. A careful reading of these scriptures and a comparison with historical facts prove what actually took place. It is a good basis for what I have called exhibit A: the nation of Israel.

Here is an example: Deuteronomy 4:27–30: "And the Lord will scatter you among the peoples, and you will be left few in number among the nations where the Lord will drive you. And there you will serve gods, the work of men's hands, wood and stone, which neither see nor hear nor eat nor smell. But from there you will seek the Lord your God, and you will find Him if you seek Him with all your heart and with all your soul. When you are in distress, and all these things come upon you in the latter days, when you turn to the lord your God and obey His voice …"

Also, read about the blessings and curses God warned about in the entire chapter 28 of Deuteronomy. I have selected this excerpt. Deuteronomy 28:1–2: "Now it shall come to pass, if you diligently obey the voice of the Lord your God to observe carefully all His commandments which I command you today that the Lord your god will set you high above all the nations of the earth. All these blessings shall come upon you and overtake you because you obey the voice of the Lord your God."

Then, later God offers a hopeful promise. Deuteronomy 30:2–3: "… and you return to the Lord your God and obey His voice according to all that I have commanded you today, you and your children with all your heart and with all your soul, that the Lord your God will bring you back from captivity and gather again from all the nations where the Lord your God has scattered you …"

This is the great promise of gathering the people again from all nations where they were scattered.

In the Old Testament book of Nehemiah God promised to regather the Jewish people after their Babylonian captivity. Nehemiah 1:8–9: God promised to regather the nation of the Jews after the Babylonian captivity. The prophet Nehemiah prays to God saying, " Remember, I pray, the word that You commanded Your servant Moses saying 'If you are unfaithful I will scatter you among the nations; but if you return to Me and keep my commandments and do them, though some of you were cast out to the farthest part of the heavens, yet I will gather them from there and bring them to the place which I have chosen as a dwelling for My name."

Yes, the Jewish people were indeed scattered throughout the world for their unfaithfulness to God. They were unfaithful to God even before coming into the great land God had promised their forefathers. Hear the lament of this knowledge in Psalm 106:26–27: "Therefore, He raised His hand in an oath against them to overthrow them in the wilderness, to overthrow their descendants among the nations, and to scatter them in the lands."

In another verse of this same Psalm a cry continues. Psalm 106:47 "Save us, O Lord Our God, And gather us from among the Gentiles, to give thanks to your Holy name and To triumph in your praise."

However, even earlier in Israel's history, the prophet Isaiah wrote in Isaiah 43:5–6 that God had promised to regather His people. "Fear not, I am with you; I will bring your descendants from the east and gather you from the west; I will say to the north, 'Give them up!' and to the south 'Do not hold them back!' Bring my sons from afar and my daughters from the ends of the earth …"

Isaiah 54:7–8 further foretells of God's heart and intention toward Israel in this promise to regather them after their dispersal: "'For a mere moment I have forsaken you but with great mercies I will gather you. With a little wrath I hid my face from you for a moment, but with everlasting kindness I will have mercies on you.' Says the Lord, your Redeemer."

Isaiah 66:8 prophetically states, "Can a nation be born in a day?" Yet the story in these last days is exactly that. In 1948, after World War II, the nation of Israel was declared the Jewish state and in one day that historic land was reinstated for Israel. The prophecy from thousands of years prior came true, down to the accurate detail of being born in just that one day!

Here are some additional references for further study, which are by no means exhaustive:

- ✍ Jeremiah 2:11—the explanation of Israel's sinful behavior
- ✍ Jeremiah 18:17—God's warning of scattering the people
- ✍ Jeremiah 31:10—the promise to regather the Jewish nation again
- ✍ Ezekiel 11:17—the promise to regather from all the other nations where they were scattered
- ✍ Ezekiel chapter 36—Israel and the Jewish people regathered, making Israel an inhabited land again
- ✍ Zephaniah 3:9— the promised restoration of the "pure" language, Israel speaking their ancient Hebrew language again
- ✍ Zephaniah 3:19–20—the regathering

So What?

Whether you agree with all the politics of the events in history or not, you must admit what is precisely foretold very clearly in the Bible. God, through His prophets, said it would happen. It did. Though some of Israel's land has been in dispute, since the end of World War II and after winning the 1967 war, this tiny nation has regained most of her original boundaries as set forth in scripture. This is truly amazing! At this time, under the Trump

Administration, the US embassy has designated Jerusalem as the official capital of Israel.

Though Hitler's diabolical attempt at genocide for the Jews failed, the hurtful hatred and rhetoric of anti-Semitism continued after World War II to this very day. We see an increase in anti-Israel political leanings, terrorism, and threats by Israel's neighbors. Rockets and missiles attacking Israel on a daily basis is commonplace. This tiny nation continues to draw persecution and scorn from the many who are opposed to it, as well as the avid attention of the whole world. Every day, we see headlines of terrorism and factional disputes over land and resources. Israel's enemies have stated their desire to wipe the Jews off the face of the map. Nations around the world are at their wits' end trying to determine how a peaceful solution can be found as fighting over this tiny piece of real estate continues. Meanwhile, any attempt at peace has resulted in continued terrorist attacks by Hamas, Hezbollah, ISIS, and others.

But take courage! God has a plan. He will fulfill His plan for this tiny nation even while other nations try to scheme and form alliances against her. God has preserved the Jewish people against all the plots of man to destroy them. History tells of deliverances from Egyptian slavery, Haman's gallows, the Nazi genocide, Herod's infanticide, and modern terrorism. God has preserved them through it all. He will defend them. He will show

His glory to them and to the whole world. One day, they at last will know that He and He alone is their promised Messiah, not only their Savior but their hoped-for Deliverer and King as well.

Example 2: Who Knew?

Daniel and the King's Dream

One book of the Old Testament is named after the young man called Daniel. Daniel was only a teenager when the destroying armies of the Babylonian Empire came against his homeland, Israel. Daniel and a remnant of the Jewish nation were taken captive during this time rather than killed because they were useful in some way to the Babylonians. In Daniel's case, he was smart, was well-educated, could read and write multiple languages, and was well-mannered, strong, and healthy. Rather than being killed, Daniel was carried off to the strange land of Babylon.

Talk about culture shock! Israel had not followed God's laws perfectly. Yet, the Jews still had many dietary and sanitary food traditions. In Babylon, many of the foods were considered unclean, even repulsive, to the Jews. It might be like any of us here in American being fed mice for supper! We could probably live on that if we had to, but we are not used to it and consider it unclean.

One event in the book of Daniel tells how the young man, along with his friends, requested a different meal plan. Remember, they were offered a chance to eat in the king's palace. *Hmm ...* That's worse than being invited to a fancy state dinner and then telling the host country's leader that the food just isn't good enough for you!

But with Daniel's humble attitude and much prayer, he suggested it could be a kind of experiment in healthy eating. Let us try it for ten days, he claimed, just fruit, vegetables, whole grains, and water, and then let the king examine us to decide whether we are healthier than those who have been eating the king's rich foods. The report was indeed favorable. Daniel had won the respect of the king!

A Bad Dream

In another event more prophetic in nature, the great King Nebuchadnezzar had an unusual and terrifying dream. He could not understand it. He felt he must know what it meant! In that culture, there were many people who practiced magical arts and fortune-telling, from soothsayers and astrologers to worshippers of various gods. They claimed they had supernatural powers and could even tell the future. Yet no one could interpret the dream or help the king understand it.

Then young Daniel requested an audience with Nebuchadnezzar, who by this time was furious with everyone. Daniel told the king that only God revealed secrets and gave wisdom. No man could interpret the king's dream; God alone could reveal the dream to the king and its interpretation. Daniel proceeded to actually tell the king what he had dreamed! The king was understandably astonished. Daniel explained further that God was trying to show the king about the future. So Daniel, the Hebrew youth, interpreted the dream for Nebuchadnezzar, the king.

This special dream and its meaning were God's way of doing several things. God showed that He alone could reveal the future. He also showed that He did so through His servant, Daniel. It also showed a powerful king, Nebuchadnezzar, that God alone was in control. The dream and its interpretation were thus written down in the king's own records for history to later see and take notice. Daniel wrote the dream and its interpretation as well. This event and the dream are recorded in his journals, the book of Daniel.

How the Lord God was proven true when the Babylonian gods (with a small *g*) were clueless! We have the records of these events then and now. For that time period, it served as a great witness to the truth and to Daniel's God of truth. Future generations like you and me can see clearly that there really is a God who knows the future.

Daniel 2:1–49 tells the record of the dream and its historic interpretation as presented in the Bible. Please read it for yourself. It is even better than my brief synopsis of it, which follows.

In short, Daniel tells the king: You saw a huge and awesome image in your dream. The head of this image was gold, the arms and chest were silver, and the thighs and belly were bronze. Its legs were iron and the feet partly clay and partly iron. A stone was cut, but not with hands. That stone struck the image on its feet and crushed the feet, breaking them to pieces. Then the whole thing was crushed together and blown away like a wind carrying away dry straw. That stone then became a great mountain and filled the whole earth.

Then Daniel told the interpretation. I will paraphrase here: You, Nebuchadnezzar, are a great king ruling over a huge empire and great kingdom. You are the head of gold. The God of heaven has given you the power, the kingdom, strength, and glory. But after you, another kingdom less powerful than yours shall come. This is the image's arms and chest of silver. A third kingdom shall arise after it, the part of bronze, and rule over the earth. Till then, another fourth kingdom, the legs of iron, will be strong as iron. But like iron breaks into pieces, so the kingdom will break into pieces. At last, the feet and toes of partly clay and partly iron will be the strength of the last kingdom. That kingdom is only partly strong and partly weak. This kingdom will be partly fragile and only partly strong. And as clay and iron do not adhere to one another, so the people of this kingdom will be mixed and not adhere to one another.

In the days of this last kingdom, the God of heaven will set up a kingdom that will never be destroyed. The kingdom will not be left to other people or kings. For God Himself will be their King. It shall consume every other world kingdom from all time and shall stand forever. And, oh yeah! King Nebuchadnezzar, this is for certain. It will happen exactly as you saw in your dream!

Well, the great king, wearing all his royal robes, fell down on his face in the royal palace and worshipped the God of Daniel! Here was the Babylonian king, Great King Nebuchadnezzar, stunned and awestruck by the power of the One True God, a Hebrew God no less! He was touched by the Almighty. He had contact with the God more powerful, more knowing, more everlasting than himself or any of his small *g* gods. This God of all Ages had just spoken through His humble servant, Daniel.

Read what Nebuchadnezzar said of this encounter: "Truly your God is the God of gods, the Lord of kings, and a revealer of secrets" (Dan. 2:4).

You will be interested to know that even secular records match the record of Nebuchadnezzar's encounter and have recorded homage to the King of Kings and Lord of Lords. Records on tablets from this period show the event. Later, the king decrees that all in his kingdom will worship the God of Daniel. This too was written down for later historians and archeologists to find. Again, the Bible proved reliable.

Further, here is what happened from what we know in historical study. The Babylonian Empire was indeed great. It is considered the most powerful state in the ancient world after the fall of the Assyrians. The capital, Babylon, had been in Mesopotamia for many years. It is dated to almost 2000 BC. The Babylonian Empire, however, fell to the Medes and the Persians during the reign of Cyrus the Great in 532 BC.

Next, Alexander the Great defeated the remaining Persians around 330 BC. This began the third kingdom sequence that correlates to the dream interpretation of Daniel. Alexander the Great was a powerful leader. The Hellenistic Age marks this time period, when Greek culture and influence were predominant. The Greek culture affected thought, law, drama, and the arts. We see the effects of this culture in the Roman Empire and in our own civilization to this day.

After Alexander's death, however, the kingdom suffered a series of civil wars. It was essentially divided into the hands of four successors—the Greeks, the Macedonians, and areas of Asia Minor as Persia and the former Median Empire. These later came under control of the Roman Empire, which was known for ironlike strength and shattering anyone who got in its way.

During the days of the Roman Empire, Baby

Jesus was born. The great King Daniel foresaw His coming onto the world scene and said that of Christ's kingdom there would be no end. His rule began with that event and continues to this very day in those who are His loyal subjects. His kingdom will one day rule over all the earth. His Second Coming will be in glory as described in the book of Revelation. His is not an earthly kingdom, as if He needed to conquer using violence or bloodshed. His is a spiritual kingdom, a kingdom of the soul, a kingship that has power to change us. One day He will reign on the earth, making all things new. You heard it first here in Daniel's vision.

Remember, however, that during the era in which Daniel lived and interpreted the king's dream, Messiah had not come yet in His first appearance. The time frame of Daniel and King Nebuchadnezzar was about 589 BC. But clearly the everlasting kingdom that cannot pass away bears distinct resemblance to the kingdom of God that Jesus talked about repeatedly. The Lord's prayer even refers to it with this phrase at the close of the prayer. The Lord's Prayer is prayed by many denominations all over the world to this day. "For thine is the kingdom, and the power, and the glory forever. Amen" (Matt. 6:9–13).

No one can deny the historic events of subsequent world powers or kingdoms after the fall of the Babylonian Empire. The Babylonian

Empire, the Medes and Persians, and Greece and Macedonia, as well as Asia Minor, under Alexander the Great stand as well-documented history. Then, after Alexander's empire was divided and weakened through various successors, the Romans Empire appeared on the world scene. Its conquest of all the known world under the Roman banner was later destroyed also. However, it did not fall to a conqueror or great leader like the other ancient kingdoms. Rome was destroyed from within through her own weakness and weak leaders. The sequence of world events matches Nebuchadnezzar's prophetic dream exactly!

Many have studied the book of Daniel for this dream and its interpretation. There is no denying the accurate description of kingdoms, empires, and events that actually took place through history. Yet, Daniel interpreted the king's dream much, much earlier than the events occurred.

Each one of these empires succeeded another. Each one fits the descriptions: Babylonian Empire, gold; Medes and Persian, silver; Macedonian under Alexander, bronze. Rome certainly fits the illustration of iron, which is strong and shatters. It can also be said it broke into pieces. The Roman Empire used its soldier strength to brutally coerce many different cultures into submission. The Jewish people were one of those. Yet, the cultures often clashed, as we see to this day.

Another God Dream

The scenario in the book of Daniel reminds me of another young Hebrew, Joseph. Joseph also had the gift of interpreting dreams. Are you familiar with the musical *Joseph and the Technicolor Dream Coat*, the theatrical version of the biblical story?

Joseph was sold as a slave to Egypt, having been betrayed by his brothers. When the Egyptian pharaoh had a dream, Joseph was the only one who could interpret it. It, like Nebuchadnezzar's, was about the future. Pharaoh needed Joseph's help to understand it. Again, in this time, God showed the pharaoh something amazing. God showed how Egypt could survive a devastating world famine and also feed many surrounding areas. Joseph told the pharaoh to store excess grain from the seven years of plenty that God would provide and use it during the hard times. Read about this in Genesis chapters 37–47.

How Do I Interpret This?

Don't miss the big picture here. I am giving you some concrete examples that clearly demonstrate that there is truth in the pages of the Bible. Let me say it again. God did these things. It was God who intervened in world history, helped kings, stood with His servants, and gave us insight into the future. Who else would know these things but God Himself? How could anyone understand what would happen centuries in the future? Who but

God knows what will happen with world powers thousands of years before the events take place? Who would know what dream you had last night? Or care? Or know with certainty where you will be tomorrow?

No one but God can. And that is my point. Only God can do these things. He wants us to know Him. He wants us to understand that prophetic Bible descriptions have proven to be true. He wants us to know that He has revealed what is absolutely true. Only He, God, knows and holds the future.

Example 3: Jesus, the Fulfillment of Prophecy (or Who Is This Guy, Anyway?)

Many other prophecies in scripture contain references to the coming Messiah. These prophecies have been described with extreme clarity. Many of them have already been fulfilled with the first coming and appearance of Jesus.

For example, there is the exact statement that Jesus made while he was hanging on the cross being crucified: "Father, why have you forsaken me?" was a statement noticed by the Roman soldiers standing guard as well as the disciples. See Mark 15:34 and Psalm 22:1. The fact that the cry in Psalm 22 was of the Messiah was an accepted idea for the Jewish people.

Even the soldiers who put Jesus on the cross unwittingly fulfilled the plan of God. The Roman guards and soldiers gambled for Jesus's garment just as was foretold in Psalm 22:18: "They divide my garment among them, and for my clothing they cast lots."

Mark 15:24 describes the event at the crucifixion when Roman soldiers divided Jesus's garments: "And when they crucified Him, they divided His garments casting lots for them to determine what every man should take." The prophecy in Psalms was written hundreds of years prior. Jesus had no control over this. The Roman soldiers were actually fulfilling prophecy. Only God could have known the exact details of the future for this event.

The prophecy in Zechariah 9:9, which was referred to in Mathew 21:5, points out a humble Messiah making His entrance into the holy city of Jerusalem. Jesus did this as described in Old Testament scripture, choosing a young donkey to ride upon rather than a victorious white horse, normally symbolizing conquerors and kings. Jesus also chose to enter the city at the preparation of Passover. He knew full well that His purpose was to be Israel's true Passover Lamb, the One waited for over the centuries. All others were merely a type or symbol, a foreshadow of the Christ. Blood of lambs and goats cannot take away sin. But God's plan of a Savior would. He would offer Jesus, His Only Begotten One, His body and blood, as payment for our sin. He prepared the way for all of us to be forgiven and receive new life. These concepts are plainly described in both the Old and New Covenants. "The Son of Man did not come to be served, but to serve and give His life as a ransom for many" (Matt. 20:28).

Didn't I Tell You?

It is calculated that there are more than 330 prophecies of Christ in scripture. These prophecies clearly describe where the Messiah would be born, that His ancestry and family lineage would be from King David, and the purpose of His coming. It is undeniable that the prophets foretold correctly. Many of these prophecies describe even the gruesome death by crucifixion that Christ would suffer. Crucifixion had not been invented at the time these prophets wrote. Yet, they clearly described the piercing of the Messiah's hands and feet as well as the excruciating pain and other details that describe His death. Isaiah chapter 53 is one of the descriptions of Christ. Another vividly detailed prophecy is Psalm 22; verses 16–18 state: "They pierced My hands and My feet; I can count all My bones. They look and stare at Me. They divide My garments among them. And for My clothing they cast lots." When compared to the actual eyewitness account of Matthew's Gospel, recorded in chapter 27:25–45 and also in Luke 23:13–45, the astounding details of Old Testament prophecy and their fulfillment in Christ Jesus is nothing short of mind-blowing!

Do the Math

Now let's do the math. In mathematics, there is a way to calculate probability. There is a formula, or algorithm, for that. So, if we take the probability of even eight of the 330 prophecies of Christ being fulfilled or proven true by just one person, the probability is hard to comprehend.

Here is a glimpse of what that probability would look like. Suppose we could cover the state of Texas in silver dollars two feet deep. One of those silver dollars we will mark with your initials using a permanent marker. Now, think about this. What is the probability that you will find that particular silver dollar on your very first try when you skydive somewhere over the state in an airplane, landing at random in Texas? Not sure? Mathematically speaking, if you calculate the probability of this event and compare it to having eight of the 330 Bible prophecies about Christ proven true, you have the same calculation. It is a probability of finding your initialed silver dollar on the very first try skydiving over Texas. Same odds. Ten to the eighty-fourth power or ten multiplied by itself eighty-four times. This number is ten with eighty-four zeros! Think of this! That means there is only one chance in 10,000,000,000 ,000,000,000,000,000,000,000,000,000,000,000,0 00,000,000,000,000,000,000,000,000,000,000,000 other possibilities. Not at all likely, right?

Yet, this very unlikely probability happened

already for us to see, and it was foretold about Jesus in the Bible. Only God, who knows all things future, past, and present, could do this. He did it so we would believe.

There are many prophesies that also describe Jesus's Second Coming. Yeshua Himself foretold this event. In Matthew 24:36–42, there is a detailed description of what Jesus tells His disciples concerning this, the times toward the end of the age, and so forth:

> But of that day and hour no one knows, not even the angels of heaven, but the Father only. But as the days of Noah were, so also will the coming of the Son of Man be. For as in the days before the flood, they were eating and drinking, marrying and giving in marriage, until the day that Noah entered the ark, and did not know until the flood came and took them all away, so also will the coming of the Son of Man be. Then two men will be in the field: one will be taken and the other left. Two women will be grinding at the mill: one will be taken and the other left. Watch therefore for you do not know what hour your Lord is coming.

Jesus gave his disciples hope to help them focus. He gave them a task to complete. He also provided a description that theologians can use even today to chart the times.

God provided deliverance from sin through the Messiah to all people. This was accomplished by Jesus's death on the cross. God provided life and power to live for Him by Jesus's resurrection. One day, God will provide a new heaven and a new earth as Jesus sets up His kingdom and reigns with those who love Him.

But first, Jesus's last command, called the Great Commission, told the disciples what to do until that time, the time of His Second Coming. He said we are to go and tell, teaching everyone in His name. This is recorded in Matthew 28:18–20: "All authority has been given to Me in heaven and on earth. Go, therefore and make disciples of all nations, baptizing them in the name of the Father and of the Son and of the Holy Spirit, teaching them to observe all things that I have commanded you: and lo, I am with you always, even to the end of the age."

This is a poem I have written that expresses the feeling many have as they question and search for understanding about God.

Kathleen Wood

Original Poem

If there really is a God out there,
What does it matter to me?
I need to know;
I do not care,
Unless He loves me so.
If that is true
Then I am His
And He is mine, you see.
Not just for living my life now
But for eternity!

3: Wait, There's More! *The Bible and the Sciences*

Archeology

We already mentioned this branch of science earlier in our introduction. Archeological digs have unearthed many discoveries that reveal credibility in the ancient biblical accounts. The Bible's accounts have been shown to be accurate in records of culture, traditions, people, and places.

Archeologists have unearthed many of the ancient cities that are mentioned as far back as Abraham in Ur. This has given credibility to what the Bible tells us about key events and figures, especially for the early patriarchs. The importance of this for biblical scholars, and for us today, is that we know the accounts in the Bible, even the very early accounts, are historically valid and have proven reliable time after time in great detail.

Kathleen Wood

Hittites, Horites, and Horror

The Hittite Culture

One example is the Bible's mention and description of a culture known as the Hittites. The Bible provides great detail about their culture, the gods they worshipped, their kings, and the geographic area where they lived. They were apparently enemies to the Jewish people. The Bible records many accounts of battle. There is even mention of names of specific kings in the Bible's accounts. The Hittites were supposed to have occupied the land of Canaan.

There used to be a debate about the biblical record concerning the Hittites. No records, other than the Bible, had been found. At that point, it was thought to be false, a made-up story. However, in 1906 archeologists discovered a Hittite capital and culture approximately ninety miles east of Ankara, Turkey. Much additional information was then revealed. We now know that the Hittites did live in the area known as ancient Canaan, just as the Bible said. The Hittite's rule had extended to Syria and Lebanon also. The Hittite capital city of Boghazkoy fell around 1200 BC. Scores of additional documented evidence in large archives were left by the Hittites, all of which coincides with biblical accounts. This civilization recorded events that tell the same story as the Bible, with similar details.

The Horites

Another example of biblical accuracy can be found in the study of the Horite civilization. The Horites were descendants of Esau. According to biblical records in Genesis 36:20 and Deuteronomy 2:12–22, they were rebels. They broke away from following the Lord God. This Yahweh God was worshipped by their forefathers, Abraham and Isaac.

The Horites were relatives of Jacob, who had received the name Israel. But Jacob's descendants gave birth to Christ through Mary, the mother of Jesus, while Esau was Jacob's estranged brother. It is a sad but true account in the Bible about deception, the quest for power, tragedy, forgiveness, and a culture that has affected history even to this day. Read the brothers' story in Genesis chapters 27–37.

Until modern times, no specific information about the Horite culture had been discovered archeologically, other than what was found in the Bible. So skeptics thought it to be completely fabricated. However, a Horite culture was in fact discovered in 1995. The Horite capital was found beneath the modern city of Tell Mozan, which is where Syria is located today. This would have been the precise location described in the Bible.

A Worldwide Flood

You may have heard when you were a young child about Noah and his ark of animals that God preserved during a worldwide flood. The great flood, it is said, covered the face of the whole earth. Only Noah and those in the ark with him survived. This is indeed the account of Genesis chapters 7–8.

What is significant is that there is evidence to support the biblical story. Similar accounts of a great flood are found throughout the world. The Gilgamesh epic is one archeological discovery from a Babylonian king. Tablets of baked clay tell the story of a great flood and a hero who was told to build a ship and take animals along and who also used birds to determine when the waters had receded from the land.

The ancient Sumerians kept lists of kings dating back to 2100 BC. These were discovered near Mesopotamia, a very early cradle of civilization. The lists are divided into two groups of kings: those who ruled before a great flood and those who ruled after.

Also notable in the discoveries about the flood are the differences in life spans recorded. According to biblical accounts, life spans were much longer, even by hundreds of years, prior to the great flood on earth. Life spans decreased dramatically on a gradual basis after the flood account. Read this in Genesis chapters 4–16.

To Conclude

Again and again, findings in the study of archeology have authenticated or proven the accuracy of biblical accounts. Records of kings, genealogical information, lists of officers who led troops or died in battles, and other major events and facts of history such as famines, floods, etc., are recorded in the Bible. They have also been recorded by various cultures on tablets dated back centuries before the birth of Christ, discovered through archeology. These discoveries make it clear that the biblical records were indeed extremely accurate and authentic to the least detail.

Would you expect anything less if the record in the Bible claims to be from God? Would you suspect that a God who is perfect, all-knowing, and completely true would do anything other than provide truth? We need to be aware of the findings of archeological science if for no other reason than to consider the accuracy the Bible's claims. Consider that it can hold truth in other areas also.

Biology and The God of Life

For many years, science has assumed that the evolutionary theory espoused by Darwin and others must be true. Based on what Darwin himself wrote, organisms change through mutation and adaptation, developing from simple to more complex forms. These assumptions have been taught to students in textbooks from elementary school to university. Students are shown drawings of the evolutionary process for mankind from animals. No "missing links" have ever been discovered. Timelines depict how evolution was supposed to have happened beginning billions of years ago starting from apes and into humans in steps of progression. But these are only drawings of what might be imagined to have happened.

The trouble is that recent scientific evidence does not support this evolutionary analysis. Instead, current evidence refutes it. Creationism, young earth, and intelligent design theories are replacing outdated science, particularly since advances in technology and equipment make new investigations possible.

When we look at gaps in the evolutionary theory, there are just too many missing links to be plausible. No one has ever discovered a "between species" that can be provided as evidence to show the theory of progression. Though we know that some adaptation within a species occurs, scientists are stepping away from supporting an overall macroevolutionary theory to explain the origin of all life.

In addition, evidence of forgery has been found in several supposed apelike creatures and early man replicas based on what evolutionary theorists claimed to be proof. These turned out to be false, man-made replicas for display, created from other bones and skulls of animals, not early man as described. The evolutionary models did not hold up to increased scrutiny of their claims.

The DNA Blueprint

Further, the discovery of DNA and the DNA "blueprint" debunks Darwin's theories even more. By his own writing before his death, he admitted that if it were ever discovered that the smallest of organisms were complex rather than simple in form and process, evolutionary theory would be proven completely false.

Yet, this is precisely what modern scientific studies in biology are revealing! The complexities of even the most minute single cell organisms have proven so complex in process and form that scientists are baffled. They have discovered that even the simplest organisms have a complex blueprint and systems beyond human comprehension. Even skeptical scientists are standing back in amazement to learn the intricacies of a DNA blueprint for life with written codes that tell our cells how to function, reproduce, heal, and exist. Much more about the genetic blueprint, genome science, and bioscience will unlock life mysteries in the near future. Research of our DNA continues to hold scientists in sheer awe.

The Bible claims that God created all things. Genesis chapter 1 tells us He created them to reproduce according to their own kind or species. A whale, for example, will always produce another whale in the natural world, never a dog or a bird. Plants even reproduce after their own kind according to their genetic blueprints. A peach tree will always produce only peaches, never plums or apples or blackberries. One kind does not evolve into another, though changes in environment may cause adaptations within a species to some degree.

There's an App for That

Because we can now "unlock" life's mysteries, moral and ethical implications are everywhere Shall we manipulate our genes to avoid diseases that are "scheduled" to appear somewhere in our lives? Shall we add genes to a human genome to make humans more like animals in some ways? Is it ethical to kill another human being and use his or her organs or genes to save the lives of those who can afford such medical treatment?

The Bible has much to say about how humans should treat one another. It is not unreasonable to imagine that our future depends upon a consistent application of moral conscience in order to use scientific and medical innovations in the best interest of humanity, the environment, and the world.

The Bible describes a Creator God who informs us how His design will run smoothly. He gives us the moral law and guidelines so that we can have successful futures and enjoy His creation.

It's All About You!

Think of it! You are amazing! With your own complex DNA blueprint, you do not have to tell yourself when to breathe, when to form new tissue, or when to secrete enzymes to digest your food or hormones to grow. All this and more is written in your unique "code." It defines you alone. No other individual has exactly the same DNA blueprint as you. Your blood carries a record of every single ancestor in your genetic history. Your skin pigmentation, eye color, hair color and texture, facial features, and hand size are all written in your genes. Even your talents and tendencies, how your brain functions, and your health are genetic at least in part as scientists continue to study what makes you the way you are.

How much we are affected by our environment and how much is genetic is still a question. Yet, God already knows. God has designed us. Therefore, when the Bible says, "Be not wise in your own eyes. Fear the Lord and depart from evil. It will be health to your flesh and strength to your bones" (Prov. 3:7–8), He is telling us that He understands how you are created better than anyone else. He knows how we function and how to keep us working at the peak of wellness.

The collection of writings called the Bible claims that it is God who gave certain people the insight to write about Him in His creation and the revelation of Himself to His creation. It reveals understanding by the writers of things not yet known at their time. Is there a factual reason to think this kind of God can know all about you? Your desires, your hopes, your purpose in life, your dreams, and your fears? Can God see us in our mothers' wombs as the Bible describes? If this is true, what does it mean for your life now?

Hear these words from the Bible penned by the song writer and king, David.

> I will praise you; for I am fearfully and wonderfully made; marvelous are your works; and that my soul knows very well. My substance was not hidden from you when I was made in secret and curiously wrought in the lowest parts of the earth. Your eyes did see my substance, yet being imperfect, and in thy book all my members were written, which in continuance were fashioned, when as yet there were none of them. How precious also are thy thought to me, O God! How great is the sum of them! (Ps 139:14–17)

According to this portion of scripture, God knows you so well that He knew you even while you were being formed in your mother's womb.

He saw that genetic composition being knit together quietly over the nine months it took from conception by your biological parents to your birth.

The Wonder of Blood

Your blood is wonderful! It traverses throughout your body, cleansing you continually from impurities. It brings life-giving nutrients and delivers healing, energizing oxygen to all your cells and organs. It rushes through your body, doing its amazing job even while you are enjoying restful, recharging sleep, apart from your conscious direction. It carries all your important information: what you ate for dinner last night, how old you are, what color eyes your dad had, and how long you will live. It even knows if you have an infection before you or the doctor do. Your blood has the information that could produce another exact copy of you. Cloned organs have already allowed people to live longer and have hope from kidney failure and other diseases.

So is it possible to imagine what the Bible says about Jesus's blood? The blood of God's own Son has special healing properties. These properties are declared plainly in scripture. Here are just a few examples:

    ✿ "How much more shall the blood of Christ who through the eternal Spirit offered Himself without spot to Go cleanse your conscience from dead works to serve the Living God?" (Heb. 9:14)

⚔ "But if we walk in the light as He is in the light, we have fellowship with one another and the blood of Jesus Christ His Son cleanses us from all sin." (1 John 1:7)

⚔ "You were ... redeemed ... with the precious blood of Christ ..." (1 Pet. 1:18–19)

God's claims, according to the Bible, are based on what we already know to be true and on what we understand about blood: it cleanses and gives life. The special qualities of Jesus's blood are worth considering.

Did He create you? Did He equip you with certain abilities, gifts, talents? Does He love you, as the Bible says? And if so, does this God of the universe really want a relationship with you and with me? If these other things about the Bible are true, could this also be true? Could He have provided for your healing, not only from disease but also from the effects of sin? Are we being given a second chance to be made in His image, the image of His dear Son?

The Bible in Geology

There are many reasons to be interested in the geological record. Geology can give us insight into what happened in the past. Areas of the Earth's surface reveal events such as floods, earthquakes, volcanic eruptions, and erosion from wind or water. Geology, along with archeological science and historical study, can give us a good picture of past events. These studies can also give us information about future events. We can learn of possible seismic activity of earthquakes, underground sources of oil or natural gas, aquifers, and what lies deep beneath the oceans.

Geological records confirm a worldwide deluge, or flood, just as described in Genesis chapters 7 and 8. One fact that shows this is that there are fossils of sea life where seas have never been. Logic tells us that sea life was washed far into these inland areas when flooding as described in the Bible occurred. The areas also contain unusual large rock formations as if sand were piled up and left to harden over hundreds of years after the water receded. The fossils of sea life signify sea water rather than freshwater rivers and lakes. Layers of rock in areas of the Grand Canyon, for example, show that at some time sea water, rather than river water as some evolutionist try to explain, was in the area. Many geologists claim that at one time the entire earth was in fact covered in sea water, just as described in the biblical account.

What Anthropologists Tell Us

What is even more amazing is that

anthropologists have found that virtually every tribe and culture has a story of a worldwide flood or deluge. As explained earlier in this book, this suggests that an event like this did occur. Anthropologists claim that this worldwide flood story is universal to all cultures on earth, even though some details vary. Variations are to be expected if written records were not preserved or where information was transferred from one generation to the next through oral tradition over thousands of years. Some historians have found historic writings and records referring to a hero. This hero, like the biblical Noah, preserved animal life by taking them aboard a large ship. Other records refer to one who tested the subsiding of the waters by using a dove, as Noah did in Genesis 8:11. For more on this amazing flood story and how God cleansed the earth, started fresh, and preserved life in a new hope, read Genesis chapters 6–8.

Other Scientific Information that Verifies the Bible

Here is a reference noted from the book of Job, dated as one of the oldest books of the Bible. It describes stars as singing. "When the morning stars sang together..." Job 38:7 Scientists now know that stars do in fact emit sound waves or sing! How could Job have known? This knowledge was only recently discovered by astrophysicists studying the cosmos. Yet Job, through the Spirit of God, told about it.

Job also noted that there are depths of the sea fed by fountains. This, again, was only a recent discovery using advanced technologies that can study previously unreached ocean depths. They have found great caves and underground fountains that fill into the surrounding waters of the seas. See Job 38:16. Also see Jonah 2:5 and chapter 6. But Job did not know. He said they were words from God Almighty.

What of the investigations of the Bethlehem star? Scientists claim there is a real possibility that there actually was such an event. Using computer simulations of the celestial bodies during that time, scientists have found that several planets convened in such a way that it is likely they would have formed a very bright light. Heavenly activity such as this would have interested and amazed the wise men, star-gazers, who were actually the astronomers of their day. The planets would have told a celestial story of a child born to a virgin, a child who would be a great king from the tribe of Judah born in Bethlehem.

Or what about the amazing verses in the Bible that describe the earth being a circle rather than flat (Isa. 40:22)? For centuries it was thought that a flat world could have caused sailors to literally fall off the edge if they voyaged too far out a sea.

Science has since discovered that this is not the case and that the earth is shaped like a sphere.

Again and again, we find the information, descriptions, and verses of the Bible reliable on these accounts, though I do not claim that the Bible is a book of science. I mention these examples to show that even in minute detail and scientific information, the Bible has been proven to be true. Would a God who cannot lie give us anything less?

What an amazing book the Bible is! Even if you don't approach the Bible as a believer, you will find its truths a relative source of help to you in your daily life. Many through the years can testify to this. Yet, I encourage you to find out for yourself. Give this amazing book a chance to change and enrich your life. Find what the God of the universe has in mind for us, what He has prepared for your life, and how to find a relationship with Him.

The Bethlehem Star

Another fascinating discovery could be the truth to questions about the star of Bethlehem. According to Frederick Larson, the star may have been a very bright light caused by a convergence of planets. This convergence appeared in the constellations that signified to the wise men the birth of a king.

Using computer simulation models, Larson was able to trace celestial bodies in their rotations through the heavens back in time to the birth of

Jesus. Using this computer analysis and comparing it with the details in scripture, he found that such a convergence would have been seen in constellations of Virgo and Leo, signifying to the ancient stargazers that a king would be born. Also significant was the fact that this king would be from the tribe of Judah, causing the wise men, who were the astronomers of their time, to take notice. The king would be of Israel!

Further, the new bright "star" would have first appeared for the wise men to see from their locations in possibly Iraq, Asia, and Africa. Then the light would have appeared to move or travel, leading the magi along. After inquiring from Herod what the prophets had foretold of this promised king, the wise men were led by the star to the young child after a period of time, though not the manger where he was born. The computer simulation fit this scenario very well, precisely as the Bible describes in Matthew chapter 2.

You can view the documentary of the star of Bethlehem for free on YouTube at www.youtube.com/watch?v=u7YTE7WFB6Y or buy the DVD version called "The Star of Bethlehem" which is available. Both provide a detailed explanation of the science behind the notorious guiding light of Christmas!

4: The Resurrection of Christ

References in this section have been provided by well-respected and meticulous scholars, authors, and apologists over centuries. Both secular and biblical records exist regarding Jesus's resurrection. There is no doubt that Jesus was crucified and died at the hands of Roman authorities. For the two thousand years since, researchers and scholars have studied and sought the truth about what followed that event. I have listed resources for your further study also.

The resurrection of Christ is key to understanding Christianity. It is also key to understanding the Bible as a whole.

There is no doubt among reasonable and reliable scholars or historians that Jesus was a real person. He lived and died. Many documented writings exist proving that others, besides believers, attested to these facts.

Jesus could not have swooned because of the tremendous loss of blood at the time of his beatings prior to being hung on the cross, as some critics think. Many witnessed the death of Jesus, including the Roman soldiers. It was their job to make certain the prisoners on the crosses used to crucify them were in fact dead and did not merely faint before they allowed their bodies to be taken down. To accomplish this, they broke the legs of their victims. It prevented the victim from pulling himself up to breath. His lungs would fill with fluid.

The reports about Jesus show that there was no question. He was obviously, without a doubt, already dead. There was no need to break His legs to cause death. However, a Roman soldier inserted a spear into Jesus's side. Out of this wound came blood and water, proving the victim's death by what is now known by medical science as "the broken heart syndrome." In this case, the heart ruptures or literally breaks. Is this not interesting? Jesus, the Son of God, died of a broken heart.

Jesus was a real person, not a mere myth or story or legend, not a made-up concept. The debate begins, however, when we look closely at who Jesus actually was, why He came, and what He did. If Jesus rose from the dead in bodily form after His death on the cross and burial as Christian believers claim, then it is important that we know this truth. Because if He did, it proves that Jesus was divine.

It also proves that only God could do such a

tremendous thing. It proves that Jesus indeed came from heaven in human flesh to us. It proves that Jesus's words were more than human words. It proves that everything He said and everything He did was from divine authority.

If God raised Jesus from the dead, it proves He was who He and others said He was, the divine Son of God. It proves the great love Father God has for us. Think about this. God sacrificed or gave His Only Begotten Son for humankind.

Who Jesus was and what He said matters. In comparing the religions of the world, not a single one claims that their leader rose in bodily form from the dead. Christianity stands alone making this claim.

Questions for Further Thought

- ⭢ Why would someone who lived more than two thousand years ago matter so much now?
- ⭢ Why are people from every background and nation still talking about Jesus Christ?
- ⭢ Was Jesus only a good teacher or a helpful person as some claim? How would you know?
- ⭢ If Jesus changed the world by His life, death, and resurrection, what does that mean for you today?

Kathleen Wood

Let's reverse the argument for a moment. If Jesus did *not* rise from the dead, what would that mean? If Jesus did not rise, wouldn't someone have His bodily remains? Think about the pressure from the Jewish religious leaders and the Roman authorities to quickly quell any question of resurrection. Surely someone would have produced Jesus's dead and bloody body! That would have silenced any claims that Jesus was alive.

Yet, we find the opposite. Neither the corrupt Jewish leaders who hated Him nor the Roman Empire with all its power and authority could produce the dead body of Jesus.

Through joined forces, the Jewish and Roman leaders leveled a massive purge and persecution effort toward believers who were making claims of Jesus's resurrection. Yet, they could not at any time find the dead body of Jesus. Jesus's disciples would not and could not deny what they had seen, the risen Christ! They refused to deny what they believed, even under penalty of prison, dismemberment, torture, or even death. They would not renounce what they said they knew to be the truth. No one could produce the dead body of Jesus. Yet many claimed they saw Him alive!

So ask yourself this: Why would the new believers risk their lives or the lives of their loved ones for something they knew was a lie? If they were making up a story or lying for whatever reason, wouldn't they give in to pressure to save their lives eventually? Wouldn't they, at least some of them, agree that this was a very weird story to keep telling? The believers would have no reason to hold on to such a story and every reason to cave and admit it if it was all just a hoax.

Some imagine that Jesus's followers were hallucinating when they said they saw Jesus after death. But psychologists know there are no group hallucinations. Such dreams or visions and imaginings are highly individual. There is no evidence that even a drug could produce the exact same hallucination for all members of a group. So the facts are not on the side of hallucinations or imagined resurrection tales.

Tortured for Truth

Lord Fox's Book of Martyrs is an excellent book that tells about the extreme torture the followers of Christ went through. The apostle Peter, for example, was crucified upside down, claiming he was not worthy to be crucified right side up like the Lord. Saul, who was called Paul, became a Christian by his own eyewitness account of the risen Christ. He endured many imprisonments, stoning, and persecution for his faith. Why if it were not true? John, Jesus's close friend and disciple, was boiled in oil. Then, as this did not kill the apostle, he was banished to the lonely isle of Patmos to live out his remaining days.

So we see that if Jesus rose as the Bible

describes, He was more than just another good teacher, leader, or even prophet. If He rose, then He is the very Son of God, as the Bible claims. It matters. It matters to every man, woman, child, and individual on Planet Earth.

What a great God who would actually manifest His life in the form of a man, come from heaven to earth, and walk among us in flesh and blood as we are to show us what God is like. Yes, that matters. We need to know if this happened. You and I need to know for sure.

Authenticity of History

Researchers and historians use clear criteria for determining authenticity of written records. Here are some criteria consistently used by scholars to verify authenticity:

- *Multiple independent sources*—the account is reported by more than one unrelated source.
- *Eyewitness testimony*—the report is a primary source, meaning a reporter was actually present during the event.
- *Coherence*—reports from multiple independent sources agree on details of the event.
- *Dissimilarity*—reports from multiple independent sources vary slightly because

of perspective and may include details other reports do not, but they do not change significantly any key details or events.

๛ *Early reporting*—the sooner a report is given, the more credible it is.

๛ *Attestation by an enemy*—if an enemy attests that the same key facts happened, credibility increases.

๛ *Embarrassment*—embarrassing details in reports lend credibility.

๛ *Aramaic substrata*—do the nuances of the Aramaic language change any significant meaning of the report?

๛ *Motivational reasoning*—what is the reporter's motive? What does the person writing such an account stand to gain?

Following these guidelines for authenticity, let us examine the resurrection accounts. The resurrection of Christ in the Bible and precise details concerning it are reported in the Gospels of Matthew, Mark, Luke, and John. These disciples were eyewitnesses.

The accounts document what Jesus's disciples saw, heard, and experienced while walking, talking, and eating with the man Jesus. After resurrection, Jesus appeared to his disciples and later to more than four hundred people, which they reported and described.

The disciples did not leave out how they did

not understand. They wrote about their emotions and how they felt. They told how they did not believe and how they became convinced, and they reported events in this authentic way.

Historians and investigators like the police or FBI say that this fact alone—the authentic reporting of the disciples to explain even embarrassing details—supports that the witnesses are telling the truth about what they saw.

The book of Acts continues where the Gospel accounts leave off. Acts documents the spread of the good news that Jesus, the Messiah, had come and saved them from sin, just as the ancient scriptures foretold. The miracles and problems they faced because of this was world changing.

It is the pinnacle event of all history. Formerly, we divided time this way. BC meant "before Christ" and AD was Latin for "the year of our Lord." However, today certain powers and political elements have made attempts to change this to BCE, or "before the common era."

Consider

If the Christ of scripture indeed has power over death as Acts 2:24 says, if the facts recorded in scripture are true as John 21:24–25 says, that means Jesus has power to change your life.

He can do what no one else can do. He can renew your spirit, heal your soul, heal your heart, heal your mind. Know this. Many have attested that He can and still does these very things!

If the claims and events as described in the Bible are valid, it is important to consider their meaning to us. Consider who Jesus is.

What does God say He wants of us? How can we have a relationship with Him? How can we know Him?

He says He created you (Gen. 1.27). He says He loves you (John 3:16). He says He has made a way to forgive and receive you through Jesus (Eph. 1:7). He says He is your Heavenly Father and wants to adopt you into His family forever (Gal. 4:1–7).

Does it, would it, change your life if it were true?

Eyewitness Accounts

The Bible claims that many others were eyewitnesses to Jesus's birth, life, death. They saw Him alive after He was crucified. Let us consider their firsthand accounts objectively through the standard criteria for authenticity.

The Embarrassing Details

Think of this. You are riding your bike with your best friend. While you approach the intersection, your friend completely loses it and falls off his bike. He might have a broken arm or something. But instead of helping him or even getting help, you just go home. You are telling the story to someone else now. If in your own account you tell that person that you just left your friend on the ground when he was hurt and ran out of there as fast as you could, leaving your friend to suffer alone, how shameful! It is embarrassing. Who would ever want you for a friend? Is this how you treat others, leaving them alone when they need your help?

Your retelling of those events would certainly reflect poorly on your character and popularity it seems. But at least you were honest enough to admit it.

That you told the truth about the event lends to its credibility. Your report is authentic because if it were not absolutely true, you would certainly not be willing to tell it that way.

Well, the disciples of Jesus gave accounts that were often embarrassing to them. They all ran away and forsook Jesus in his hour of need. They were afraid of getting arrested or killed by the same Romans or religious leaders who were arresting Jesus. They actually hid out after Jesus was crucified. They feared being next. They hoped no one would find them. Everyone already knew that they were Jesus's disciples. They must have thought, *They killed Jesus. They will be looking for us next!*

They were actually hiding when the women reported Jesus's resurrection the Sunday morning following His gruesome death. Back in that male-dominated society, the Middle Eastern cultures, women were thought to be subservient to men. A woman who knew more about what Jesus was up to than they did would not be acceptable. If Jesus revealed Himself to a woman first rather than His own disciples, well, this was surely a shame to them! Yet, Mary had the first look at the resurrected Lord, according to scripture. And because of this, she was assigned by Jesus to tell the others, the men, the amazing news.

The disciples didn't believe the woman's report at first. They thought she was crazy, making up such an incredible story! *How can such a thing happen? You are beside yourself, woman!*

But as the truth of her story came to light, it must have been completely embarrassing to the disciples. These embarrassing details help authenticate that the disciples were in fact telling the truth about these events.

Later, Jesus appeared directly to a disciple named Thomas. Thomas did not even believe the other disciples. He said he would never believe it unless he saw the Lord for himself. He said that the story of a resurrected Jesus was just too impossible to believe. Thomas saw Jesus hanging on that cross and watched him die a terrible death. He saw the soldiers pierce Jesus's side to make certain He was dead. No way could He be alive after all that! Thomas refused to believe, he said, until he could put his own finger in Jesus's nail-pierced hands and actually touch the side where he had seen the soldier spear Jesus. He could not believe the incredible story even if the others were convinced of it.

But Jesus came directly to Thomas. Scripture says Jesus came into the room when the doors were shut. He told Thomas to go ahead and put his hands in His side where he watched the soldier stab Him to make sure Jesus was really dead. He said, "Feel where they placed the nails in my hands and feet. See. Now believe."

Thomas was stunned and amazed. He fell at Jesus's feet in worship. Thomas confessed, "My Lord and My God!" And right then and there Jesus gave a special blessing to all the rest of us. He said, "Thomas, because you have seen me, you believe; blessed are those who have not seen and yet believe" (John 20:29).

Eye Spy

Another interesting fact about the Gospel writers is that they wrote their accounts with details that were unique to each's own perspective or viewpoint. Eyewitnesses do this. If you are standing behind a building when an explosion goes off, for example, you see and would report what you saw from that angle. Your report would include some details that someone standing in a different position might not have noticed. Another eyewitness might be in a car traveling past the building when it explodes. He will report what he saw as he was passing the building. You both saw the explosion, but chances are that you have some details the other person does not and vice versa. You each see the event but from a different viewpoint.

This was the case with Jesus's disciples. Some skeptics will use the variation in detail between the Gospel accounts to claim that the reports conflict. Actually, the variance lends to their credibility! The main events do not conflict. They are certainly the same. But some details are different because each of the Gospel writers—Matthew, Mark, Luke, and John—see and experience the events from different perspectives or viewpoints.

The apostle John remembered the account of Jesus speaking to him from the cross while he was there with Mary, Jesus's mother. So he included that detail when he wrote (John 19:25–27). It was significant to him. Matthew does not mention it at all, however. Does that make it less true? No. This is an example of John's personal eyewitness account from his own viewpoint. Matthew mentions details that were equally important from his perspective. He traces the lineage of Christ through Adam to Noah and then to Abraham, showing that Jesus is the direct descendant of David according to genealogical record (Matt. 1:1–17). The other disciples do not mention it.

Not a Game!

Much of the New Testament was written during the first century after Christ. Some were as early as thirty to sixty years after the Resurrection. These are what historians call "primary source" records, which are considered the most reliable and accurate reports. They were the first accounting from the time the actual events happened.

Therefore, the accounts of Christ were *not* like the party game of Telephone, where participants whisper what they think they just heard, possibly even filling in the gaps to make sense, and then whispering that version of the original story to the person down the line. We laugh hysterically with this game because there are inevitably alterations and mistakes to the original statement. However, significant details about Jesus were written down and recited in particular form like the lyrics of a song. These were used in group meetings to rehearse and promote beliefs, keeping the truth pure, free from error, and unchanged.

These are known as Christian creeds or catechisms. The earliest of these appeared shortly after Jesus's death and resurrection, only three years in fact! The apostles were still alive. Also still alive were those who experienced His many miracles and healings, as well as those who saw Jesus after His resurrection. More than four hundred witnesses who saw Jesus ascend into the heavens as stated in Acts 1:3–11 were still alive.

Apostle Paul's letter to the Corinthian church contains such a creed. Scholars and historians have long accepted that at the time Paul wrote this letter, AD 60, early creeds were already used as part of Christian gatherings and meetings. These were sung as songs or chanted in order to keep major beliefs free from error and preserve basic Christian doctrine. These orally rehearsed doctrines and writings are the earliest recorded and most reliable Christian creeds.

Please see these in detail:

> For I delivered unto you first of all that which I also received, how that Christ died for our sins according to the scriptures; And that he was buried, and that he rose again the third day according to the scriptures: And that he was seen of Cephas, then of the 12: After that, he was seen above five hundred brethren at once; of whom the greater part remain unto this present, but some are fallen asleep. (1 Cor. 15:3–6)

Another valuable part of the creed appears earlier in this same letter from Paul to Corinth: "But there is but one God, the Father, of whom are all things, and we in Him; and one Lord Jesus

Christ, by whom are all things, and we by Him" (1 Cor. 8:6).

Again, this statement was transferred from Paul to Timothy, a second-generation disciple of Christ, dated AD 62–66: "… without controversy great is the mystery of godliness: God was manifest in the flesh, justified in the Spirit, seen of angels, preached unto the Gentiles, believed on in the world, and received up into glory" (1 Tim. 3:16).

This concept stating belief of the divinity, humility, death, and exaltation of Jesus as Christ is basic to Christian doctrine and is found here:

> "Let this mind be in you, which was also in Christ Jesus: who being in the form of God, thought it not robbery to be equal with God, but made Himself of no reputation, taking the form of a bondservant, and coming in the likeness of men. And being found in appearance as a man, He humbled Himself, and became obedient to the point of death, even the death of the cross. Therefore God also has highly exalted Him and given Him the name which is above every name, that at the name of Jesus every knee should bow, of those in heaven and of those on earth, and those under the earth, and that every

tongue should confess that Jesus Christ is Lord to the glory of God the Father." Phil. 2:5-11.

Important to Know

Scholars agree that Philippians 2:5–11 was written only in AD 52–62, after Paul's visit to the church in Philippi. We see, then, that not enough time had elapsed for the accounts to become tainted or altered as would be the case in legend or folklore. That happens over hundreds of years and several generations. But with the New Testament scripture, not enough time had passed for additions or deletions to occur. The original reports in early creeds were preserved within the first generation as well as recorded through writing.

Therefore, the transfer of these doctrinal beliefs about who Christ is, what He came to earth to accomplish, and how we can attain heaven through Him have been preserved. These creeds and teachings are still in use today in many churches and denominations throughout the world. An authentic Gospel message has been successfully preserved through the generations as a testimony to what God has done.

Councils and Creeds

Later councils of Christian leaders have decided to include the significant beliefs of these early creeds in their doctrinal statement. These are also still in use today. The Apostles' Creed and the Nicene Creed are two examples.

The Apostles' Creed was adopted in the first century by a council of Christian leaders as a statement of faith based on the early apostle's teachings in scripture. When the original apostles passed, this creed stood the test of time and is still in use today, centuries later. Churches using the creed include Catholic, Eastern Orthodox, Anglican, and many Protestant denominations.

> "I believe in God, the Father Almighty, Creator of heaven and earth. I believe in Jesus Christ, His only Son, our Lord. He was conceived by the power of the Holy Spirit and born of the virgin Mary. He suffered under Pontius Pilot, was crucified, died, and was buried. He descended to the dead. On the third day He rose again. He ascended into heaven and is seated at the right hand of the Father. He will come to judge the living and the dead. I believe in the Holy Spirit, the holy

Catholic Church, the communion
of saints, the forgiveness of sins, the
resurrection of the body, and life
everlasting. Amen." Apostles Creed

Please note that the reference to the holy
Catholic Church here in the creed does not refer
to the denomination of Catholics necessarily. That
denomination or hierarchy did not exist at the
time the creeds were written. Rather, it refers to
the universality and brotherhood of all Christian
believers everywhere through all time, often called
the church universal.

The church, or the fellowship in faith, for all
of those believers in Christ across the world and
through all generations holds true to these basic
doctrines. Their faith is called the fellowship of
believers based on these doctrines, which have
been passed down through the centuries since
Christ's first appearance on earth.

A similar creed adopted in AD 325 in Turkey
was called the Nicene Creed. This creed is used
in Oriental Orthodox and Assyrian churches,
according to Wikipedia. It contains a statement of
beliefs consistent with the Apostles' Creed.

Another interesting creed to note is from the
apostle John. John taught a disciple, Polycarp,
who was instrumental in converting another
person, Irenaeus, to the Christian faith. Irenaeus
later became the church's regional leader in Gaul,

which is now Lyon, France. During the late second century, Irenaeus developed his Rules of Faith to counteract many of the controversies arising from false teachers and false doctrine. The Rules of Faith were true to the original statements set forth in the Apostles' Creed but were written to clarify the basic Christian beliefs and their doctrines. This was meant to guard against heretical teaching, which was creeping in at the time.

As you can see from the statement, it emphasizes the triune nature of the Godhead (i.e., one God expressed in three persons—the Father, the Son, and the Holy Spirit—and the unity or agreement of these three in one purpose. This could be a difficult concept to understand if it were not explained properly, particularly if one is coming from a culture that believes in more than one god.

It is possible that the doctrine of the Holy Trinity, or triune nature of God, is the most difficult to understand. It may seem to conflict with the idea revealed in the Old Testament or ancient scripture and recited by Jewish ceremonies that reads, "Hear, O Israel: the Lord our God, the Lord is one!" Deuteronomy 6:4

However, God is one just as the simple chemical composition of water is H_2O. It does not change its chemical composition just because the temperature reaches the freezing point. Water may turn to ice, yet it is still H_2O. We can see that water becomes a gas like vapor carried by clouds, yet it remains water. Our God is the same God throughout all of scripture, even in His manifestation of Christ and giving of His Spirit to those who believe.

In this Nicene Creed, we see the explanation for the Godhead mentioning the Father, Son and the Holy Spirit as one:

"I believe in one God, the Father Almighty, Maker of heaven and earth, and of all things visible and invisible. And in one Lord Jesus Christ, the only-begotten Son of God, begotten of the Father before all worlds; God of God, Light of Light, very God of very God; begotten, not made, being of one substance with the Father, by whom all things were made. Who, for us men and for our salvation, came down from heaven, and was incarnate by the Holy Spirit of the virgin Mary, and was made man; and was crucified also for us under Pontius Pilate; He suffered and was buried; and the third day He rose again, according to the Scriptures; and ascended into heaven, and sits on the right hand of the Father; and He shall come again, with glory, to judge the quick and the dead; whose kingdom shall have no end. "

The Persecuted Church

Another piece of evidence in favor of the resurrection of Jesus is the intensity of persecution His followers endured. The Roman government,

Kathleen Wood

which was supported by the ruling religious leaders, persecuted the disciples and anyone else who believed the new faith of Jesus and believed in Jesus as the Son of God. All these original disciples were martyred. Others, even centuries later, are still facing severe persecution and death for their belief in Jesus. We know this from historical accounts and secular sources, not merely from accounts described in the scriptures.

Ask yourself, if you were facing torture or death over a story you made up, wouldn't you cave in to pressure? Wouldn't you spill the beans and confess, "Yeah, sure, we made it up"? Especially if you had loved ones and family who were being tortured as well? Your persecutors would say, "Just recant your faith in Messiah Jesus. The story that you are telling about a resurrected Savior, just give it up!"

But if it were true, if you actually saw Jesus alive after His death, if He changed your life, if He truly demonstrated that He is the King of Kings and Lord of Lords, if someone you knew and loved were healed in some way by Him, how could you deny this?

Most of the early Christians chose to be martyred and suffer the loss of family and friends rather than recant their faith in Jesus. Many more were imprisoned. And many Christians are still being persecuted today. Persecution of Christians is actually on the rise.

Yet, Christianity has thrived throughout the

centuries because of what we know to be true about God: Christ is eternal. It is truth. He not only did as He said He would do, rising again, but He is coming back for us just as He said He would.

Jesus Christ will come back as judge. He will judge the earth in righteousness. He will reign on the earth a righteous reign of peace and true justice. He also promised that we shall reign with him in glory, all who believe, even though we have not seen as these early disciples did.

In Conclusion

Ask yourself, if the Bible has been shown to be accurate, a collection of very old manuscripts with information that is now verified through scientific fields of study such as archeology, geology, history, and others, what does that mean in terms of the authors' knowledge?

How did they know these things thousands of years before the discoveries were actually made?

What did the authors themselves say about this?

If the Bible were true, what does that mean for you?

Who did Jesus say He was?

What did Jesus say about His own death before it happened?

Who do you say Jesus is?

What is the implication for your own life?

My prayer is that Jesus's own words from John 8:32 will become true in your life and that "… you shall know the truth and the truth shall make you free."

References and Sermon Notes

Archeology and the Bible, materials compiled by Larry McKinney, Dan Masler, John Monson with photography from The British Museum, London, Oriental Institute, University of Chicago, Museum of Anatolian Civilization. Rose Pub. 2002 Torrance CA

Answers to Skeptics Questions, Evidence for the Resurrection. RW Research, Inc. Rose Publishing 2004 Torrance CA

Answers to the New Critics, Why Trust the Bible. Bristol Works, Inc. Rose Publishing 2007. Carson CA

A Time Line of Key Events in the History of the Bible, How We Got the Bible. RW Research, Inc. Rose Publishing 2008, Carson CA .

Decision Magazine, managing editor Pierce, Jerry, "The Towering Truth of the Resurrection", article April 2017, BGEA Charlotte NC

Decision Magazine, managing editor Pierce, Jerry, "Biblical Archeology" article April 2017 BGEA Charlotte NC

Ehrman, Bart D. *The New Testament—An Historic Introduction to the Early Christian Writings*, 216, 262. New York: Oxford University Press, 1997.

Engram, Steve. *The Why, How and What of the Resurrection*. Desert Springs Community Church, Sermon Notes April 2017. Goodyear AZ

Engram, Steve. "Who God Is." Sermon notes, August 16, 2015 Goodyear AZ.

Engram, Steve. "The Importance of Studying Prophecy." Sermon notes, June 7, 2015. Goodyear AZ

Eternal Productions. "101 Scientific Facts and Foreknowledge" Updated/accessed September 2019. http://www.eternal-productions.org/101science.html

Evidence for the Resurrection. RW Research, Inc. Rose Pub., 2004. Torrance CA.

How We Got the Bible - A Timeline of Key Events in the History of the Bible with contributions from Michael Cochane, Philip Comfort, Timothy Paul Jones, Erral Rhodes, Lawrence Scrivani.. Rose Pub 1998 Torrance CA

Hunt, Dave "In Defense of the Faith, Biblical Answers to Challenging Questions". The Berean Call 2009 Bend OR. http://www. thebereancall.org.html

"Jesus - Fact or Fiction?" DVD by DC Media 001, May 2011 featuring Brian Deacon, directed by Peter Sykes. Reasonable Faith. http://www. reasonablefaith.org.html

Larson, Bob. "Star of Bethlehem" documentary www.youtube.com/watch?v=u7YTE7WFB6Y

December 2013, DVD by Shadow Films 1971.

Lashua, Pastor Rob, Desert Springs Community Church http://www.dscchurch.com, DS Apologetics, classes and notes, "The Resurrection of Jesus Christ", accessed September 2019.Goodyear AZ

Lashua, Pastor Rob, Desert Springs Community Church. April, 2017, "Smart Faith Conference": with contributions from Marty Clapp, Woody Gant, Trevor Schalow, James Umber. Conference

Notes and references: Josephus. *The Jewish War.* 7:203. Cicerio. *Against Verres.* 2.5.169. *Tacitus Annals.* 15:44. *Lucian.* 115-200. Pontius Pilate, *Annals* 15:44. Talmud, Sanhedrin. "Mara Bar Serapion 43a." Letter at the British Museum., Eusebius, Church History, Book 1V, ch15:4

Ludemann, Gerd, *The Resurrection of Christ—An Historic Inquiry,* Amherst, NY: Pometheus Books, 2004.

McDowell, Josh. "The New Evidence That Demands a Verdict". Thomas Nelson Pub. Nashville TN 1999.

Morris, Henry M. *The Biblical Basis for Modern Science.* Master Books, div. New Leaf Pub Grp, Inc. Green Forest AR, 2002

McKinney, Larry, and Dan Master. *50 Proofs for the Bible.* Peabody, MA: Rose Publishing, 2007.

Old Testament, Archeology and the Bible. with contributions from Professor Larry McKinney, Dan Masler, John Monson. Rose Publishing 2002 Torrance CA

Old Testament, 50 Proofs for the Bible, contributions from Hoerth, Dr. Alfred, McKinney, Larry, Masler, Dan, Monson, John. RW Research Inc. Rose Pub. 2007, Torrance CA

On the Physical Death of Jesus, article – Journal of the American Medical Association #255 (March 21, 1986, p 1457)

Strobel, Lee. *The Case for Christ: A Journalist's Personal Investigation of the Evidence for Jesus.* Grand Rapids: Zondervan, 1998.

Wallace, Warner. *Cold Case Christianity – A Homicide Detective Investigates the Claims of the Gospel,* Colorado Springs: David Cook, 2013.

Geisler, Norman L., and Frank Turek. *I Don't Have Enough Faith to be an Atheist.* Wheaton, IL: Crossway Books, 2004. See chapters 9–11.

Wright, NT. *Was Jesus raised from the dead? Did he really die or only pass out? "* video lecture Accessed Sept 2019 http://www.youtube.com/watch? v=yBNr9hjN5WYg

About the Author

As a student of Sociology and Psychology in her undergraduate years, Kathleen was passionate to learn about cultures and people from every background. Later, earning a degree in Elementary Education from Eastern Michigan University, she focused her attention on teaching a new generation of young people. With a master degree in Reading and Literacy, Mrs. Wood has taught over twenty years in professional education helping many students become successful readers, writers and thinkers.

Having traveled throughout the U. S. and the world in Ireland, France, Belgium, England, China and Africa, Kathleen Wood has also prepared other teachers in team training programs.

Now retired, Kathleen lives in Alabama where

she enjoys her sunny days with her daughter, son-in-law and three grandchildren.

"It is my hope that through this writing, many young people will come to know that there is a great big God who loves them and cares. This knowledge gives purpose and meaning to our lives. It is hope for a new generation. This is the light in the darkness."

Printed in the United States
By Bookmasters